Vallum

J A Elcock

A first edition of 100 copies

Published by The Artel Press in 2018

ISBN 978-0-9926035-2-6

Cover artwork by the author

Printed in the UK by Imprint Digital

For MH.

CONTENTS

By the same author

Come, Thule
The Northern Biochemist

The idea for this collection emerged following a visit to the Isle of Bute and an opportunity to visit St Blane's Chapel. The ruins of the monastic foundation are approached by foot and lie in a remarkable landscape whose unique topography and sense of place was clearly understood by those early settlers.

I also had in mind however somewhere more local, a stretch of railings separating woodland from an adjacent suburban street; sometimes the boundaries between the secular and spiritual worlds are not always that obvious.

That sense of other, of a place apart, informs much of the work included here.

These poems I hope will also show that we may do well to observe the behaviour of birds whose inherent understanding of these boundaries is so fascinating.

They show the way, but you have to be willing to listen.

J A Elcock

SANCTUS

VALLUM

I see my skin fascinates..
a wintry parchment of mottled greys.
In its inescapable truth be glad
that you are observer,
and I remain, observed.

Yet 'twixt me and thee
a flicker of days have passed.
My age, perhaps will be your fate?
So too, to wrestle with weak limbs
and sail closer to the wind of death.

Such forces steer me ever closer
to a nearing horizon.
And for this be thankful:
that I too, am glad.

For my purpling temple is a gift
that only us of age receive,
a token of our passage
from this world to the new.

I am as was, a mere vessel.
Delicate winds caressed my hair,
kisses would blow me
nearer to harbour.

You are the children
sitting on the bowsprit
and happily waving,
in the bliss of youth.

1

Our shore is certain
for this body, a vallum,
whose skin is vellum
for the journey written there.

CONVERSATION AT UIST

I am well-willowed,
cleft in the green shoot,
pinned by oak-gloved clasp.
Fingers nailed by thorn bushes
in their warp and weft,
my breath transpired, swept seawards,
to be whorled by woodland winds -
for my spirit lies lost (in the drowning).

But you will hear me in the corncrake's rasp
blown from beached glass berthed in the bothy,
or wombed in the booming roar of the geo.
Lucky too, to hear the grated fall of notes
of a hand fumbling on the muffled latch...
yet your browned mouth gapes wordless
and buried in the peat of Ness.

CAPE WRATH

Your latitude is bitter to swallow -
for rocks aggrieve the throat,
and salt offends my tongue.

A promontory of ancient descent,
your aggressive visage juts
inquisitively, into a breathless sea.

As one who instils apprehension,
your mere proximity arouses fear,
for greened teeth bite deep in the black!

My voice is soon swallowed in your eddies,
blue lost in grey, diluted in tin.
Howled into blackness surrendering to your name.

Your mollusc'd waist embraced,
I blithely scrape my tethered wrists
against your well-honed shore.

ON GARSTON SANDS

Why the Heron shriek?
Out of the ether,
Phantom-like, the voice of the dead
Thrust unheard from the throat of the living.
Lost in the marram,
Fleeing the advancing tide.
Yet heard, for one,
To wonder at the spring
From whence the craw came forth.
The neck, so lithe,
Snake-like for enfolding hands to grasp
And grimly squeeze,
Just as advancing waters grip the sand
To wrench a lurking roar
From this mercuric land.
I hear you, but do not understand.

SEVEN DAYS DRAWING

Grenade
whistle
steeple
hand
stone
cell
Sword

MASSACRE AT LUNT

See, the filthy shawl that was Badger,
broken by the roadside.
Fox, trammelled,
her yawning mouth in unending yelp.
Gull, transformed to bloodied fan,
or one bloated, now a shriekless ghost.
Carrots, crushed by the wheel
spill their orange blood.
Mistle Thrush, lies stunned
and felled by madness.
Rabbit?
Hangs eviscerated from Tree.

A CLATTERING OF JACKDAWS

Valley.

Roar
Jet
Flush
Clatter
Flock
Craw
Silence

Valley.

KITCHEN LANDSCAPE

Sleep long fled the bedroom
on a path now vague, the stairwell blocked
by the jumbled mountain range of chairs.

So I must look out across the kitchen table
past a Corian lake of glacial green,
where dishes tumble as some vast moraine.

And a strip-light sends its silent lightning
into the echoing valley of the hall.

Alone in the wilderness. Night.
The distant jet lends a civilising air,
an abrupt click - and the fridge's hum
brings it quickly down to ground. (No one hurt).

Meanwhile I have to sit
by the glowing embers of the kettle,
while Artex clouds hang heavy above my head.

The silence too is not so silent,
for pops and creaks emerge fox-like
from the caves in the floor
and ghosts in the freezer do their moonlit work.

At least the morning glimmers through the sodium lights
and the tap drips with a promise of rain.

Yet I must with weary tread, go back to bed
and climb the wooden hills, again.

A LESSON IN HISTORY

Pressburg
Crestfallen
Crook hollow
Crick willow
Wood Warbler
Will 'O' The Wisp
Priest Hole
Tub thumping
Conscience pricking
Blind fever
Bliss heaven
Bread leaven
Blood harbour
Bratislava

RUABON SHORE

THIS IS
THISTLE
COTT A
RU A B
PHORP
27
ORRELL
THE
CCRI NGTO
HISTLE
PHORPRE

THIS IS
THISTLE.

COTT A
RU, A B?
PORPHYRY

27
ORRELL

THE
 CCRI NGTO
WHISTLE
PHORPRE.

APUS APUS

From Damselfly to Swift
is of one incarnate from the other.
So seamless in transition
is your morphology of ingested form,
of utility into beauty.
From an insect, most altruistic of beings,
to a bird, who simply screams for more.

HEAP'S MILL

Slack-bound on its cleat,
a rope waits with unhurried sleep
and swings benignly
of its load, unbecoming, unknown.
Heavy the hemp strands sit sodden,
and knock the bulwark of bull-nosed bricks
longing for a sure grip to heft it
heavenwards, bring life to what is else
lifeless, disengaged.
If I were to light you, fuse-like,
would you yearn for the immolation
to free you from the burden of the once-was mill?

ON PASSING

I let an ageing mirror to the deep,
and watched it bolt stag-like from my grasp
drawn, like one possessed, clear out of sight.
Slipped under the silvered surface of the sea
it returned from whence it came,
its cold hand jabbed into distant, sandy shore.

What, but madness could direct its flight?
Driven by longing for the dark
it sliced an erratic path
through its new and unsuspecting home.
A mere flash, then gone.
No chance to mourn, or curse the fickle hand
that surrendered it from this world to the next.

And the light that once it threw
with such alacrity about the room,
is quickly snuffed by the icy gloom.
Time faltered and healed, in its passing.
A once shining face erased,
and furrowed brow revealed.
With brief pursed lips
the surface bid you, gone.

SANCTIOR

MATTHEW 18:20

At the Scrape, I bow,
for this is a hallowed place,
and one made holy
by the ribs and vaults of birds.
What joy to be enthroned *in Cathedra*,
cocooned in the stalls of a youthful copse!

From the timbered nave
a busying congregation of garrulous duck
bears witness to the joyful winter sun.
Flocks of finch enact a daily rite,
the cormorants raise their arms in prayer
and a wagtail dips its slender beak into the font.

HYMN

SEA

Save Us, Star of the Sea,
maiden of the riverhead.
For we are grounded on the sand
and beached by our perdition.
Thaw me with your distant light
just as a creeping wick eats time
by slow degrees, to warm a groping hand,
a heart, assimilated with
the movement of the sea,
or a brow cleansed by seawater.

WOOD

Save Us, Moon of the Woods,
for I feel the lichen fur my mouth
and inaction tangles me in a beech's roots.
I see sky and stars,
but ivy chokes me in the blacking mulch.
Though my lips shape sounds
words are stolen by the nightjar's purr
and my heart leaps with fear,
like a woodcock bolting from its copse.

SKY

Save Us, Birds of the Fields
for though I am lost

you bring form to the empty sky
and life to the stretching earth
in the conviviality of your flocks.
Rooks reap with patience in the soil,
gulls laugh with the sheer joy of flight
and partridge crouch in the lee of the plough.

DEAD DUNLIN

My brothers! Hear me.
    Wind whittles foreshore reeds

Brothers, hear me!
    Sand scours weathered plucking post

Your sweet voices sing softer.
    Rain cloys shaking ash keys

I wish you nearer.
    Moon-drawn water mires the roost

My bill tires from our endless bowing.
    Cold leaches warmth from the willow sap

Yearning to preen my tail, I fail.
    Death-knell of Curlew calling

Friends, you fall off in the distance.
    Rushing tide harried by wind

Sleep comes.. yet I see grey light?
    Black clouds drip with needling rain

Pity me brothers, for my wings stay furled.
    Beetling flock, flashes with brilliance

How cold this water on my wind-worn flank.
    Sea kisses, caresses, claims

THE WHITETHROAT

Dawn came, felled the streetlights with its axe,
revealed you in the hedgerow.
Your steady eye
impenetrable, knowing..
piercing, as if to the heart of the cosmos.

Your shattering song lords over the yarrow,
to strike one dumb.
To drown a presumptuous tongue
dog-like in gaping mouth,
in a wan face shamed by ignorance.

Your cascading trill of throated command
centres-all, would weld one to the place.
But faltering feet fail, fall fallow,
flit - flown.
A divine encounter, gone.

A POEM FOR JOE

O bitter shame of homeward stare
from storefront bleached by city lights,
the bags that groan with goods of busy lives.
And then to pass with downcast eyes
to see you Joe, sat frozen in the gutter
brings welling flames of crass regret
to feel the warmth lie there
emanating, somehow from your tiny frame.

THE BLACK CURLEW

Steam leaches from the furrow's grasp,
and men trudge a well-trod way, work-wards
to till the sleeping ground.
Here fields, well-birched slope elsewhere;
and unknown waters sidle seawards,
giving birth to ever greater shores.

The pitch and toss of hoes
lend a lonely rhythmic pulse to the lifeless ground.
Hour succumbs to hour, the sweat of well-versed hands
strives to waken sleeping seed.
A robin shivers, crows laugh at the straining men,
else, winter stops all mouths
and the yeoman farmers labour on.

With stooped backs, all sackcloth-bound
they plunge arms earthwards, and rise
with supplicating hands of clay,
then delve again to tease the frozen soil.

So too, in nearby rutted field,
with purposeful yet prayerful pace
birds steal the morning's share, dip there,
and soft *cur-lee* accompanies the walking herd.
Marsh Grouse, most lonely, lovely, bubbling bird!

But here with sweeping wings of gilded bronze,
a stranger lands cast not, but out of, jet.
Journeyed, yet not weary,
as Jordan's rivers, so too the fields of Hale.

A regal bird and one who humbles in the preening,
one sent as messenger, who prepares the way.
His brothers bow with scarce a glance
to dig again in the black earth.

THE DREAM OF ST NICK'S

Herring gulls tend graves,
Knives fly from drawers
To mint lead coffers with their blades
And the ground yawns to yield its dead.
See, the steeple falling
To rise triumphant
Rebuilt before my eyes.
Soft, the sound of a girl's choir
Voiced *sotto* in Shaw's Alley.
As the ship breaks free of the nave
To sail beyond the organ loft,
Shades pass unnoticed
Where waves now lap at the fountain.

DOMINE SALVAM FAC FLORENTINA

I am the sound of boots breaching the tower,
of brickwork glazed in the shrieks of laughter
frescoed by time,
imperious to open skies.

Of boys, bellowing in the race,
for the blue smoke distant on the river
and the first to know the name
and Line therein.

I am the ruddy faces of the climb,
of sugared fingers pressed to glass,
a coal dust cough
through gleaming teeth.

Tho' silenced by the winter years
when the cold light fell as rain,
I rise with joyful cry
for the Dingle lighthouse shines again.

ENCLOSURE

Things shared, such are unseen:
long corridor to an empty room,
street glimpsed from ancient woods,
ground where blood was shed.

That, which is inexpressible, expressed:
moulding leaf of circling oaks,
smell of damp in a basement room,
a distant garden from a Carmelite cell.

NEWINGTON

Precious the trestles, well-washed
on which the years have long laid down,
and mirrored faces there, well-met.

Chairs, unchanged, that grate full-well
against the wooden floor that slumbers still.
Warm words drift loftwards and hug the voilet beams.

Only a numbered yell may pierce the fug.
Cut and thrust of cutlery? Mere splashes of sunlight.
A waitress? The hoot of an owl.

Without, withal, all-loved,
unbroken, immutable, immobile.

How then the hand that holds the twilit pen?
My face that stares, autumnal?

A lengthening shadow fills the upper room.

CHIESA DI SAN MARTINO

Broken on the gridiron and
smelted in the ovens of Murano,
bells bounce off bricks of raw umber.
Gullies stream with the blood of forty martyrs
whose hands hang hewn on the altar,
and dogs gnaw at a Doge's bones.

for F.O'C

LARUS MICHAHELLIS

Perched on the fondamenta,
silent, and a stare
encompassing land and sea.

Carpaccio would have known his steely eye
at once careless, yet accusatory -
understanding me!

A Dalmatian prince, cloaked silt-grey,
whose lethargic gaze
across the lagoon of history flies.

Such purity of nape and crown
are robes as if a spotless gown,
to prick the conscience of one's breast.

To live for four or sire four thousand,
he transcends our years.
Gull, *serenissima*, a priest of birds.

From cupola to quay his leisured glides
bridge sacred and profane
and broad wings held, as on the Cross.

LAMENT

Thrown, thrown away like so much trash,
the effects of two millennia.

Slung, slung and forgotten,
abandoned in pursuit of self-love.

Lost, lost in the haste for chattels,
supplanted by whimsy and waste.

Lassus, now a voice in the wilderness,
a memory spoken in the voice of birds.

HAWK AND GULL

There is another place, outside ourselves
en plein air, and betrayed by mewing cry.
In the blue free realm, three sixty all told
where below and above are seemingly as one.

Far off, a hawk's stiff wings beat time
and correct the fragile thermals of an early March,
with geometric precision describe an arc,
then bisect it neatly to elucidate His space.

Tangentially a grubbing gull appears,
with poorly copied compass lines
and his younger brother teasing in the yard
rattling feathered sabres down below.

So disjointed in the bowl of the sky,
for what purpose and why the quarrel?
The birds alone know,
and joust unhindered in the heavens.

We may stand there, unknowing,
or ignore them, unbeknown,
speaking tongues that they know not
nor we them, understand.

SANCTISSIMUS

A CAROL

When sleep calls, sweet-heart,
And your cheek falls, warmth-wards,
To your dream land, bed-warmed,
Consider this now, great thought.

Of far lands, dust-blown,
And a place there, pink-skied sheep-land,
Where Christ lay, your Belovéd.
Many winters past, my belovéd.

A simple space, a concrete room,
Where mummy rocks, *coo-coo*, dove's tune.
Cows low, goats groan - friendly fellows!
Lambs nestle in the subtle shadows.

Heaven dips, earth-bound,
And from chiton white, a radiant light,
So wars must slumber, taking fright -
Mankind wakes, o blesséd Night!

Peace to you then, good child,
Warming quilt yearns morning light.
Christ is born, mourning ends,
Night flees from gentle Bethlehem.

SANCTUARY MAINTENANCE

Morning spills as milk, and the rising sun
grips the chimneys of the terraced street
to wash slate beaches with a yellow light.

At the red, some patient cars -
and builders vans chattering as starlings,
murmuring in chorus, at dawn.

Radios suckled by the warm dash
hum in gentle unison,
but at green the coughing has already started.

And to their disparate ways
the painted tradesmen fly,
whether home to roost or awake, I know not.

Save one, whose powdered doors
rise from pristine tail,
marked distinct from well-weathered flock.

Crepuscular too in its nature
and with such gentility on the clutch,
the driver waits with patience in the wings.

For the Transit holds a secret
behind its royal doors,
where two eyes gleam in unhurried stare.

All manner of subtle tools
is the treasure of holy comestibles
and every article of care:

Velvet gloves by which the key is turned,
a chamois skin to stroke the holy doors,
linen napkins that bite the paten dear,

hessian scrap, to wipe the chalice clear,
the wax and tabernacle oil,
censer restorative - amber too.

Only a faint scent at the lights
belies its purpose.
Of clerestory musk, perhaps.

For surely, daily the dutiful business
of sanctuary maintenance
is in our sacred groves and bowers?

A chorus of chirruping bus brakes
flushes the van from cover,
into the clay thicket of the city.

EPIGRAPH

In these three last words
So much, accomplished.
Millennia of redemption
Ennobled by it.
For ourselves, beginning,
In this a simple, peremptory,
Enabling, 'yes'.